S0-BRM-168

LIBRARY OF THE
SCHOOL OF THE INCARNATION
2601 SYMPHONY LANE
GAMBRILLS, MD 21054

Battle Ready

 Raintree · OSPREY PUBLISHING

Union Flags of the Civil War

3250000134 3780

Philip Katcher · Illustrated by Rick Scollins

This American edition first published in 2003 by Raintree, a division of Reed Elsevier Inc., Chicago, Illinois, by arrangement with Osprey Publishing Limited, Oxford, England.

All rights reserved. No part of this publication may be reproduced or transmitted in any form or by any means, electronic or mechanical, including photocopying, recording, taping, or any information storage and retrieval system, without the permission in writing from the publishers.

For information, address the publisher:
Raintree, 100 N. LaSalle, Suite 1200, Chicago, IL 60602

First published 1993
Under the title *Men-at-Arms 258: Flags of the American Civil War (2) Union*
By Osprey Publishing Limited, Elms Court, Chapel Way, Botley, Oxford, OX2 9LP
© 1993 Osprey Publishing Limited
All rights reserved.

ISBN 1-4109-0123-8

03 04 05 06 07   10 9 8 7 6 5 4 3 2 1

Library of Congress Cataloging-in-Publication Data

Katcher, Philip R. N.
  [Flags of the American Civil War. 2, Union]
  Union flags of the Civil War / Philip Katcher ; illustrator, Rick Scollins.
      v. cm. -- (Battle ready)
Originally published: Flags of the American Civil War. v. 2, Union. Oxford [England] : Osprey, 1993, in series: Men-at-arms.
Includes bibliographical references and index.
Contents: Regulation flags -- Army Headquarters flags -- The Army of the
Potomac -- Cavalry flags -- Naval flags.
  ISBN 1-4109-0123-8 (library binding-hardcover)
  1. Flags--United States--Juvenile literature. 2. United
States--History--Civil War, 1861-1865--Flags--Juvenile literature. [1. Flags--United States. 2. United States--History--Civil War, 1861-1865.]
  I. Scollins, Richard, ill. II. Title. III. Series.
  CR113.K35 2003
  973.7'41--dc21
                          2003005358

Author: Philip Katcher
Illustrator: Rick Scollins
Editor: Martin Windrow
Printed in China through World Print Ltd.

Author's acknowledgments
Thanks are due to Ronn Palm, Michael J. McAfee, Howard Michael Madaus, and Harry Roach.

Publisher's Note
Readers may wish to study this title in conjuction with *Confederate Flags of the Civil War*.

CONTENTS

UNION FLAGS OF THE CIVIL WAR

INTRODUCTION

The regimental or battery set of colors was more than simply a unit designation, issued for the ease of a commander in identifying his units in the field. It was the very symbol of the regiment; it was its heart, the thing that drew its members together. As such it was fiercely defended in action, where it flew in the center of the line, drawing enemy fire upon its carriers.

Each regiment received its colors in one of its first formal ceremonies, which itself was almost an initiation into the world of the soldier. On November 12, 1861, Pennsylvania's governor Andrew Curtin, accompanied by staff members, took the train from his capital city of Harrisburg to the county seat of Chester County to present a set of colors to the newly formed 97th Pennsylvania Volunteer Infantry Regiment. Arriving shortly after noon, the state officials were met by the entire regiment, which then escorted them to the city's court house. Following a speech introducing the

The typical flag presentation ceremony of a national color, here to a Kentucky regiment at Camp Bruce, near Cynthiana, Kentucky.

governor and his return speech to local citizens, the officials had dinner. Then, at about three, they all met at the 97th's training camp located on the county fair grounds.

There, according to the regiment's historian: "The Regiment was formed in column by division closed in mass in front of the stand, on the north side of the Fair buildings. The people had crowded around the reserved space with such eagerness as to render it difficult for the guard to clear sufficient room for the reception committee and those who were to take part in the proceedings.

"When all had been arranged, the Governor came forward, uncovered, holding the staff upon which waved the beautiful stars and stripes of the flag he was about to entrust to the keeping of the regiment, as its banner, around which to rally when led forth into the performance of whatever duty an

This national color of the 2nd Battalion, 18th US Infantry Regiment has its stars arranged in the canton in the manner of flags made by Evans and Hassall, Philadelphia. (West Point Museum Collection)

imperiled country might demand, and, in these words consigned them to the Regiment...." Curtin spoke at great length, ending with this peroration:

"It is the flag of your fathers and your country. It will be yours to bear it in the thickest of the fight and to defend it to the last. Upon its return, it will have inscribed upon it the record of those battles through which you have carried it, and will become a part of the archives of Pennsylvania; and there it will remain, through all coming time, a witness to your children and your children's children of the valor of their fathers. With a full confidence that in your hands this banner will never be disgraced, I entrust it to your care and for the last time bid you farewell."

In camp, the regimental colors flew over the unit headquarters as a guide post to members and outsiders alike. In combat, it was drawn into the very center of action where, in obedience to millions of words like those spoken by Governor Curtin at thousands of presentations, it was fiercely defended. Take, for example, the 38th Pennsylvania Volunteer

Infantry Regiment at Antietam. There the regiment was one of dozens which stormed Confederate positions in the now famous Cornfield. According to the 1865 *History of the Pennsylvania Reserve Corps*, "A most singular fatality fell upon the color bearers of this regiment. Sergeant Henry W. Blanchard, who had carried the regimental colors through all the storms of battle in which the regiment fought, was a most remarkable man. Born in Massachusetts in 1832, he was about thirty years old. He had the most complete control of his feelings; in the fiercest hours of battle, was always perfectly calm, never shouted, cheered or became enthusiastic, but steadily bore up his flag. At the battle of New Market cross roads, when every color-bearer in the division was either killed or wounded, Sergeant Blanchard received a wound in the arm, he retired a few minutes to have his wound bandaged and then returned to his place. At Antietam he was so severely wounded that the flag fell from his hands, and he was unable to raise it; Walter Beatty, a private, seized the banner to bear it aloft, and almost immediately fell dead, pierced by rebel bullets; another private, Robert Lemmon took the flag from the hands of his fallen comrade, a companion calling out to him, "don't touch it, Bob, or they'll kill you," the brave boy, however, bore up the banner, and in less than a minute lay dead on the ground; the colors were then taken by Edward Doran, a little Irishman, who lying upon his back, held up the flag till the end of the battle, and for his gallantry was made a non-commissioned officer on the field."

Few things were more disgraceful than losing one's colors in battle, and extreme sacrifices were often made to save them. For example, the 1st Delaware Infantry Regiment were also at Antietam where they were stopped by overwhelming enemy fire, suffering heavy losses. They were driven back, caught between fire from enemy troops in their front and from reinforcements who confused them for Confederates in the fog of battle. Despite tremendous fire, according to the regiment's historian: "On the ground, a few yards in advance, where the line was first arrested, lay a large number of our men, killed or wounded, and among them lay the colors of the regiment, one of which was held by Lieutenant-Colonel Hopkinson, who was wounded. Major Smyth, Captain Rickards, Lieutenants Postles, Tanner, and Nicholls, Sergeants Dunn and McAllister, with several other non-commissioned officers, rallied a large number of the men for the purpose of returning to the original line, recovering the colors, and holding the position, if possible.

"They sallied gallantly to the front under a terrible tornado of shot, and held the position for a considerable time.... When the regiment retired from the field both colors were brought with it, one by Lieutenant C. B. Tanner and the other by Sergeant Allen Tatem, one of the color-guard."

The generally accepted jargon for the elements of flags and their components is used throughout this book. The *canton* is the square or rectangle placed at the top of the flag next to the pole or staff. A *border* is the flag's edging, when rendered in a color different from that of the *field*. The main part

of the flag is the *field*. The *hoist* is the side of the flag next to the staff, while the *fly* is the opposite side of the flag. The flag is shown with the hoist on the left and the fly on the right; this is the *obverse* or front of the flag; the side seen when the hoist is on the right and the fly on the left is the *reverse*, or rear. When speaking of measurements, however, flag dimensions are often referred to as being, for example, six feet on the hoist (i.e., along the staff), by five on the fly (i.e., parallel to the ground). The staff itself is the *stave*; the metal object on top of the stave, usually a spearhead, an axehead or an eagle, is the *finial*. The metal cap at the bottom of the stave is the *ferrule*. Many flags have cords and tassels hanging from the finial; collectively, these are simply referred to as *cords*.

Howard Michael Madaus, one of America's leading experts on Civil War flags, holds an authentically reconstructed national color of the 2nd Wisconsin Volunteer Infantry Regiment, which he carried at the 125th anniversary recreation of the battle of First Bull Run.

REGULATION FLAGS

The Army of the United States basically had two colors per dismounted regiment, which were issued according to armywide regulations issued August 10, 1861. From the *Revised Regulations for the Army of the United States, 1861*:

"1436. The garrison flag is the national flag. It is made of bunting, thirty-six feet fly, the twenty feet hoist, in thirteen horizontal stripes of equal breadth, alternately red and white, beginning with the red. In the upper quarter, next to the staff, is the Union, composed of a number of white stars, equal to the number of States, on a blue field, one-third the length of the flag, extending to the lower edge of the fourth red stripe from the top. The storm flag is twenty feet by ten feet; the recruiting flag, nine feet nine inches by four feet four inches.

Colors of artillery regiments

"1437. Each regiment of Artillery shall have two silken colors. The first, or the national color, of stars and stripes, as described for the garrison flag. The number and name of the regiment to be embroidered with gold on the center stripe. The second, or regimental color, to be yellow, of the same dimensions as the first, bearing in the center two cannon crossing, with the letters US above, and the number of regiment below; fringe, yellow. Each color to be six feet six inches fly, and six feet deep on the pike. The pike, including the spear and ferrule, to be nine feet ten inches in length. Cords and tassels, red and yellow silk intermixed.

Colors of infantry regiments

"1438. Each regiment of Infantry shall have two silken colors. The first, or the national color, of stars and stripes, as described for the garrison flag; the number and name of the regiment to be embroidered with silver on the center stripe. The second, or regimental color, to be blue, with the arms of the United States embroidered in silk on the center. The name of the regiment in a scroll, underneath the eagle. The size of each color to be six feet six inches fly, and six feet deep on the pike. The length of the pike, including the spear and ferrule, to be nine feet ten inches. The fringe yellow; cord and tassels, blue and white silk intermixed.

Camp colors

"1439. The camp colors are of bunting, eighteen inches square; white for infantry, and red for artillery, with the number of the regiment on them. The pole eight feet long."

Each foot regiment was to have two camp colors, carried on the extreme right and left of the regiment by sergeants serving as general guides. In fact many of the actual colors violated regulations

The national color behind this captain appears to be that of the Governor's Foot Guard, a uniformed but strictly social Connecticut organization. Nonetheless, it shows the eagle finial which often topped the national color, and the tassels. (David Scheinmann Collection)

The national color is carried in action in 1861.
Note the eagle and streamers.

by having unique insignia on them. The 72nd Pennsylvania Volunteer Infantry, for example, had plain dark blue camp colors with a golden bee painted on a sky blue oval; and the 95th Ohio Volunteer Infantry had scarlet silk camp colors with a golden wreath surrounding the unit designation, "95 OHIO."

General Orders No. 4, January 18, 1862, said that "camp colors ... will be made like the United States flag, with stars and stripes." Surviving camp colors of the 128th New York Infantry were made in this style, with the number 128 on a dark blue cloth field, sewn onto the color.

Manufacturers' variations

The description of the national flag used as a camp color, as well as both a garrison and regimental flag in the regulations, was vague in such details as the exact arrangement of the stars in the canton. Indeed, it did not even spell out if the canton were to be square or rectangular. A variety of styles of canton shapes and star designs were seen in actual practice, varying according to the flags' makers.

One basic difference between Army national colors and flags flown by civilians and non-military governmental organizations is that most Army national colors used gold stars while most other American flags had white stars. Apparently this came about when the Army switched to silver embroidery for its stars before the war; silver embroidery thread tarnished to an unsightly black, so gold was substituted for silver – hence the gold stars. Many private manufacturers during the war did embroider white stars on the cantons of the national colors they supplied under state contracts, but Army-issued national colors had gold stars, usually painted rather than embroidered.

Army-issued national colors were provided to regiments which needed replacement colors or did not receive presentation colors from their state

The star pattern in the canton of this national color of the 18th US Infantry Regiment matches those made under a US Quartermaster Department contract by Alexander Brandon, issued through the New York Quartermaster Depot in 1864. (West Point Museum Collections)

government or local organizations. Army-issued colors were issued at the Quartermaster Depots in Philadelphia, New York, and Cincinnati, Ohio. Private contractors between May 1861 and October 1865 supplied the Philadelphia Depot with 890 national colors, the New York Depot with 917 national colors, and the Cincinnati Depot with 500 national colors.

National colors provided by the Philadelphia Depot apparently had the gold stars in their rectangular cantons arranged as a vertical double ellipse with an additional star in each corner. Some had a center star, while some lacked this final star.

New York Depot national colors had the gold stars in a square canton arranged in five horizontal rows. Until July 4, 1863, when West Virginia was admitted as a new state and a new star was authorized for it, these had six stars in the middle row and seven stars in each of the two outer rows. After July 4, 1863, each row had seven stars. Although Nevada was admitted to the Union on October 31, 1864, no star was authorized to mark that state until after the war was over.

Apparently national colors supplied by the Cincinnati Depot had rectangular cantons with seven horizontal rows of gold stars. Each row except the bottom one had five stars, with four

stars in the bottom row until July 1863, when it, too, acquired a fifth.

Most regiments, however, especially early in the war, were presented with national colors by some local group which had acquired them from private contractors. These colors were quite expensive by the standards of the day.

Pennsylvania's state inspector general asked for bids for making flags for the Commonwealth's troops from three local manufacturers. One, Horstmann, asked $160 for a pair of national and regimental colors, $35 for a cavalry standard, and $12 for a cavalry guidon. Evans & Hassall wanted $135 for a pair of national and regimental colors, $35 for a cavalry standard, and $22.50 for a cavalry guidon. Brewer wanted $110 for the infantry colors, $30 for the cavalry standard, and $15 for the guidon. (At this time a private soldier's pay was only $13 a month.)

On November 27, 1861, the adjutant general of Kentucky asked for quotes for making flags for the state's troops from both a local manufacturer, Hugh Wilkins of Louisville, Kentucky, and Tiffany & Co. of New York City. Wilkins replied: "I will make infantry regimental colors for $125 per set with the arms of Kentucky on each side of the standard and regular regimental flag stars and stripes with the number of each regiment in gold on each side and the same in the blue flag on a scroll under the coat of arms. Cavalry standards done in a like manner for $45.00 each, guidons for $10.00 each. Artillery flags same as Infantry."

Tiffany wired: "Blue regimentals both sides $100.00 each in three weeks, with case, belt, and fringe. National stars and stripes $60.00 each in one week. Guidons embroidered name and number $25.00 pair in two weeks."

Presentation national colors made by Tiffany went mostly to New York and some Connecticut units, although some were carried by Michigan units and at least one by an Indiana unit. Tiffany colors were embroidered with white stars in a square canton. Until July 1863 they were set in six horizontal rows, the middle two with five stars while the outer two had six stars. Starting in July 1863 the top three rows had six stars each; the fourth row had five; and the bottom two rows had six. Unit designations on Tiffany colors were rendered in script letters.

Presentation national colors made by another New York maker, Paton & Company, used white silk appliquéd stars set in five horizontal rows, the middle one of which had six stars while the upper and lower two had seven stars each, in a square canton. The unit designation appeared in script letters.

Evans & Hassall of Philadelphia, Pennsylvania, arranged the gold stars in the rectangular cantons of their national colors as a simple double ellipse of stars surrounding a single star in the center, with one gold star at each corner of the canton. New Jersey regiments after 1863 received national colors made by this company.

Horstmann Brothers & Co., a general military equipment and uniform supplier from Philadelphia, also produced presentation national colors for Minnesota troops for a short time starting in late 1862, and for West Virginia's troops after that state's formation. These were made like the Evans & Hassall colors with a double ellipse of gold stars in a rectangular canton. Both Evans & Hassall and Horstmann also produced national colors for Pennsylvania troops, but these differed in that the state seal surrounded by stars was painted in the center of the canton. The first national colors supplied by Horstmann to New Jersey used this same design, with the New Jersey state seal surrounded by stars in their cantons.

Maryland troops received national colors made by Sisco Bros., of Baltimore, with square cantons and, after July 1863, five horizontal rows of seven gold stars each.

Hugh Wilkins, Louisville, Kentucky, produced national colors for Kentucky troops and, apparently, units from Illinois, Indiana, and Ohio. These were unusual in that a light or sky blue was used for the square cantons. The gold stars were arranged in six horizontal rows, five in the top and bottom rows and six in the other rows.

Gilbert Hubbard & Co., Chicago, Illinois, made national colors for units from Wisconsin. Its first ones had the state seal as well as stars in the rectangular cantons. However, replacement colors made until July 1863 had gold stars in six horizontal rows with six in the top, bottom, and two middle rows and five in the second and fifth rows.

Regimental colors were also issued through the three basic quartermaster depots. Between May 1861 and October 1865 the Philadelphia Depot purchased 765 regimental colors; the New York Depot, 1,021 regimental colors; and the Cincinnati Depot, 564 regimental colors.

Many of Philadelphia's regimental colors came from Horstmann and Evans & Hassall. These colors bear the US coat of arms on the eagle's breast over a three-piece red scroll painted with a raised center section and under a double curve of stars: the top row had 21 stars, the bottom row 13 stars.

New York's Depot had a variety of suppliers including A. Ertle, Paton & Co., and A. Brandon. They had a large, but somewhat unrealistic eagle under two rows of stars, 18 in the top row and 16 in the bottom.

Cincinnati's Depot had several contractors who provided regimental colors of various qualities.

A private of the Veteran Reserve Corps, formed from men no longer capable of active field service but still capable of serving, holds one of the Corps' national colors. (Ronn Palm Collection)

John Shilleto of Cincinnati turned out well-painted eagles with detailed feathers and realistic heads. His first colors had 21 stars in the top row over 13 stars in the bottom, ending at the tail of the motto scroll. His post-July 1863 colors had 20 stars over 15 stars in two rows which extended below the ends of the scroll.

Another Cincinnati supplier, Longly & Bro., turned out eagles which were poorly painted, with ill-defined feathers and a "black eye" on each eagle's head. Until July 1863 the top row of stars on these flags had 21 stars, over 13 stars in the bottom row; after that date they bore 21 over 14 stars, the latter touching the trails of the motto scroll. The motto scrolls from both makers had lower center sections.

Hugh Wilkins' regimental colors featured eagles with down-turned heads, as well as another design which had the eagle perched on a US shield in the center of a circular clouded perch. Both had five-piece red motto scrolls.

Both national and regimental colors, save those presented by local groups and locally made, were issued without regimental designations in the stripe or motto scroll. It was up to each regimental colonel to have the regimental designation put on each color.

An officer holds a battle-torn national color bearing three battle honors for engagements in the Army of the Potomac. Note the axhead which tops the stave.

To return to the 1861 Army Regulations:

Standards and Guidons of Mounted Regiments

"1440. Each regiment will have a silken standard, and each company a silken guidon. The standard to bear the arms of the United States, embroidered in silk, on a blue ground, with the number and name of the regiment, in a scroll underneath the eagle. The flag of the standard to be two feet five inches wide, and two feet three inches on the lance, and to be edged with yellow silk fringe.

"1441. The flag of the guidon is swallow-tailed, three feet five inches from the lance to the end of the swallow-tail; fifteen inches to the fork of the swallow-tail, and two feet three inches on the lance. To be half red and half white, dividing at the fork, the red above. On the red, the letters US in white; and on the white, the letter of the company in red. The lance of the standards and guidons to be nine feet long, including spear and ferrule."

Modifications to the 1861 regulations appeared soon after they were published. The first changed the guidons issued to mounted units. According to General Orders No. 4, issued January 18, 1862: "1. Under instructions from the Secretary of War, dated January 7, 1862, guidons and camp colors for the Army will be made like the United States flag, with stars and stripes."

Mounted units wanted to fly a version of the US national flag. However, not even the modification of January 1862, which gave them a guidon version of the US flag, was enough for many such units; instead, they often flew the whole US flag. Indeed, a message from the commander of the Army of the Ohio, dated June 3, 1862, to Brigadier General Thomas Crittenden noted: "The general yesterday observed one of the batteries in your division carrying a large flag instead of a guidon, as ordered. The general desires to know why the orders on this subject are not carried out."

Battle honors

Shortly after the guidon revision order was issued a practice that had been standard for many years before the war was made official. Regiments and batteries were allowed to indicate their service in battle on their colors. As stated in General Orders No. 19, February 22, 1862: "It has been ordered that there shall be inscribed upon the colors or guidons of all regiments and batteries in the service of the United States the names of the battle in which they have borne a meritorious part." The order went on to say that "It is expected that troops so distinguished will regard their colors as representing the honor of their corps – to be lost only with their lives – and that those not yet entitled to such a distinction will not rest satisfied until they have won it by their discipline and courage."

This privilege was soon abused by a number of volunteer units which put the names of battles in which they had played the most minor of parts onto their colors. According to John Billings, a veteran of the 10th Massachusetts Artillery, in the Army of the Potomac, "Originally battles were only inscribed on flags by authority of the secretary of war, that is, in the regular army. But the volunteers seemed to be a

A color-sergeant holding his battle-torn flag. The regiment is unknown. (Ronn Palm Collection)

This national color used in Virginia in 1861 displays a different star pattern from that usually employed. There were no clear national regulations on the arrangement of stars.

law unto themselves, and, while many flags in existence today bear names of battles inscribed by order of the commanding general, there are some with inscriptions of battles which the troops were hardly in hearing of."

This was not always the fault of the troops who carried the colors; it was often unclear what unit was authorized what battle honor. Some commanders published lists of battle honors that could be placed on flags, some simply ordered every unit present at any given battle to put the honor on its flag. Even some governors issued orders to their state units to put specific honors on their battle flags.

As a result of this confusion, on March 7, 1865, the Army of the Potomac issued its General Orders No. 10 which listed every volunteer unit in the army along with a list of battles that could be placed on its colors. However, the Army of the Potomac appears to

Table A: Unit Designations

Unit designations on national colors were placed on one of the horizontal stripes, often the seventh one from the top. However, this system was far from universal, as seen by the selection of representative national colors which have survived and are listed below. When the stripe is indicated it is counted from the top down. When letters or an abbreviation follow the number or capital letters, such as "2d" or "REGt," the small letter was usually raised parallel with the top of the larger numbers and one or two dots placed under the small letter.

Unit designation	Designation placement
1st BATn PIONEER BRIGADE	7th stripe
2nd MICH. INF.	7th stripe
2d Wisconsin Infantry Volunteers.	7th stripe
3rd REGt WIS. VETERAN INFANTRY.	7th stripe
7th REGt NEW JERSEY VOLUNTEERS.	7th stripe
13th ILL.	7th stripe
15th REGt Ky VOLs	8th stripe
15th REGt WIS. VOLs.	7th stripe
15th REGt IND. VOLS.	9th stripe
18th Michigan Infantry.	7th stripe
19th REGIMENT/ MASSACHUSETTS VOLs	5th/7th stripes
MASSACHUSETTS VOLUNTEERS/21st. REGT.INFANTRY	4th/6th stripes
28th REG. PENNa VOL. INFy	7th stripe
40th REGt N.J. VOLS.	7th stripe
46th Regt. MASS. MILITIA	7th stripe
46th REGT. O.V.I.	3rd stripe
46th Ohio V.V.I.	Center of canton
51st REG'T P.V.V.	Top stripe
56th Regiment,/MASSACHUSETTS VOLs.	5th/7th stripes
60th REG'T O.V.U.S.A.	7th stripe
68th REGT. OHIO VET. VOL. INFANTRY	8th stripe
76th OHIO	7th stripe
154th Regt. NYSV (in script)	7th stripe

have been the only large organization within the Union forces to attempt to standardize battle honors and, by the time it did so, many of its older units had already been mustered out, their battle flags now hanging in state capital buildings.

* * *

Finally, according to the 1861 regulations: "The ambulance depot, to which the wounded are carried or directed for immediate treatment, is generally established at the most convenient building nearest the field of battle. A *red flag* marks its place, or the way to it, to the conductors of the ambulances and to the wounded who can walk." General hospital flags were in fact yellow, with a large green Roman letter H on the field, and smaller yellow flags with green borders were generally used to mark the way from the firing line to field hospitals. This was standardized by General Orders No. 9, January 4, 1864, which called for a yellow general hospital flag 5 ft. by 9 ft. in size with a Roman letter H, 24 inches tall, on its field. Post and field hospitals had the same flag although 5 ft. by 9 ft. in size. Rectangular guidons 14 inches by 28 inches edged with one-inch green borders were to mark ambulances and the route to field hospitals.

A color-sergeant of the 141st Pennsylvania Volunteer Infantry Regiment sits in front of the regiment's national and regimental colors. The regimental color tassel hangs over his right shoulder. (Ronn Palm Collection)

ARMY HEADQUARTERS FLAGS

No special colors were authorized under the regulations for army headquarters. Yet there was a precedent for having a special flag for marking the headquarters of a commanding general; during the War for American Independence, George Washington's headquarters was marked by an all-blue flag bearing 13 five-pointed stars.

In fact, the first flag selected to mark the headquarters of the Army of the Potomac, under General Orders No. 102, March 24, 1862, was a plain national flag. The national flag used by the army's headquarters in 1863, now in the Military Order of the Loyal Legion of the US, Philadelphia, had four rows of seven stars over a last row of six stars in its canton. It was 4 ft. on the hoist by 5fi ft. in the fly. It bears no unit designation or other distinctive marks.

Indeed, veteran John Billings later recalled that "The stars and stripes were a common flag for army headquarters. It was General Meade's headquarters till Grant came to the Army of the Potomac, who also used it for that purpose." Therefore, on May 2, 1864, the army's final commander, Major-General George G. Meade, adopted a new headquarters flag. According to an army circular issued at that time, "Hereafter the designating flag for these headquarters will be a magenta-colored swallow tailed flag, with an eagle in gold, surrounded by a silver wreath for an emblem." Billings said the guidon was actually "lilac colored." It measured 4 ft. on the hoist by 6 ft. on the fly.

The Army of the Potomac's Artillery Reserve had its own flag, authorized in General Orders No. 119, April 30, 1862. This was a 5 ft. by 6 ft. rectangular red flag with a white star in its center. This was changed by General Orders No. 53, May 12, 1863, to a red swallow-tailed guidon, of the same dimensions as other corps flags, with a pair of white crossed cannons on its center. Brigadier-General Henry J. Hunt, Army of the Potomac chief of artillery, apparently adopted a blue guidon with a red Roman letter A surmounting a pair of white crossed

This infantry regimental color conforms in overall design to those known to have been issued by the New York Quartermaster Depot. The regiment that received it would have been responsible for getting the number filled in properly. (West Point Museum Collections)

cannons for a personal flag in 1864. In October 1864 the Horse Artillery Brigade received a blue triangular flag with red crossed cannons, and the letters H above the cannons and A under them.

Other Army of the Potomac generals flew their own flags. The flag of the chief of engineers, for example, was a blue field, 4 ft. by 6 ft., with a red turreted castle, the symbol of the Corps of Engineers.

The Army of the James was created from the X and XVIII Corps in 1864. On May 3, 1864, its headquarters adopted a 6 ft.-square flag divided horizontally into red and blue halves. A large five-pointed star in white was placed in the center.

When Major-General Philip Sheridan received command of the Army of the Shenandoah he appears to have used a swallow-tailed cavalry guidon to mark his headquarters. The guidon was divided into horizontal halves, the top white and the bottom red. A red five-pointed star was placed on the top half, and a similar star in white on the bottom half. The guidon measured some 3 ft. on the hoist by 6 ft. on the fly.

Under General Orders No. 91, Department of the Cumberland, the flag for department and army headquarters was a national flag "with a golden

eagle below the stars, two feet from tip to tip." The flag's size was 5 ft. by 6 ft. However, according to General Orders No. 62, April 26, 1864, the headquarters flag was to be a 5 ft.-square national color; it bore the gold Roman letters "D.C." within the canton and a gold eagle clutching a laurel branch in its left claw and five arrows in its right. The motto "E PLURIBUS UNUM" flew from its beak. The eagle was painted on the field no deeper than the canton. The placement of the eagle is slightly different on the reverse from the obverse.

The Departments of the Army of Tennessee and the Army of the Ohio had very similar headquarters flags, both with blue fields and gold fringe, cords and tassels. The Army of Tennessee's flag had the corps badges of the XV and XVII Corps on a vertical background of red, white, and blue. The flag of the Army of the Ohio had the corps badges of the X and XXIII Corps, suspended from sabers, topped by an eagle which looked very much like the colonel's rank badge. It would appear that these two headquarters flags were adopted after they joined the forces under Major-General William T. Sherman in North Carolina in the dying days of the war.

The Military Division of the Mississippi apparently used a 5 ft.-square plain yellow flag as its headquarters flag. In early 1865 the badges adopted by the corps within the division were painted on it.

THE ARMY OF THE POTOMAC

As the Union's field armies grew in size, various commanders attempted to make units easy to identify in the field through systems of unique flags carried by each formation and unit. The Army of the Potomac's General Orders No. 102 was issued March 24, 1862, under Major-General George B. McClellan's direction, and gave the Union Army its first comprehensive army-wide flag designating system.

According to the sections which provided instructions on flags, the army's general headquarters would be marked by a plain national flag. Corps headquarters would have a national flag with a small square flag, of a different color or set of colors, on the same staff under the national flag. The I Corps flag was to be red; II Corps, blue; III Corps, blue and red in vertical halves; and IV Corps, blue and red in horizontal halves.

All divisions had the same size flags, 6 ft. long and 5 ft. wide. The first division of an army corps had a red flag; the second division blue; the third division a vertically divided red and blue flag (contemporary illustrations show that the red half was on the hoist side and the blue on the fly); and the fourth division a horizontally divided red and blue flag.

In fact, however, period writers do not mention any fourth divisions or their flags in the Army of the Potomac for the period. Colonel Charles Wainwright jotted this description in his diary only two days after the new order setting up the flag system was issued: "One of the first (orders) prescribes the powers of corps commanders, and also designates flags for each headquarters. First Division's [sic] will carry a red flag 6 by 5; Second Division's blue; Third Division's red and blue vertical. Ours being the Second will have a blue flag."

The brigades within each division were marked by different flags, each the same size as the division headquarters flag. Within each first division, the first brigade had a red and white flag in vertical stripes; the second, vertical white, red, and white stripes; and the third, vertical red, white, and red stripes.

Within each corps' second division, the first brigade had a vertical striped blue and white flag;

the second brigade had vertical white, blue, and white stripes; the third, vertical blue, white, and blue stripes.

The same sized flags were used by brigade headquarters in each corps' third division. The first brigade had vertical red, white, and blue stripes; the second, vertical red, blue, and white stripes; and the third, vertical white, red, and blue stripes.

Among corps with a fourth division, the first brigade had horizontal, red, white, and blue stripes; the second, horizontal red, blue, and white stripes; and the third, horizontal white, red, and blue stripes.

Within each brigade, each regiment was to carry in addition to its national and regimental colors a copy of the brigade headquarters flag with the numbers 1, 2, 3 or 4 on it, according to the unit's ranking on the brigade table of organization. White numbers were used on colored bars and colored numbers (which often appear to have been red) on

The color guard of the 36th Massachusetts Volunteer Infantry Regiment hold their well-worn colors in this picture dating from late in the war. The two general guides hold their camp colors on either end of the line; these would have flown at either flank of the regiment to mark its position. (US Army Military History Institute)

white bars. Actual regimental flags measure between 54 and 56 inches on the hoist and between 70 and 72 inches on the fly.

Artillery batteries were to carry the colors of the division to which they belonged as well as a right-angled triangular flag 6 ft. long and 3 ft. wide at the staff. Cavalry units were to have the same as the artillery, although their flag was to be swallow-tailed. Engineer units had a white disc of a diameter equal to one third of its width on the flag of the division to which the unit was assigned.

The Regular Brigade had a white star on a red flag, the regimental number being in the middle of the star. This was changed by General Order No. 119, April 30, 1862, to a "blue flag with a white star in the center." In fact, an original flag carried in the brigade is at the Chapel of St. Cornelius the Centurion, Ft. Jay, New York. It is only 18 inches long on the hoist and 3 ft. on the fly, with a white star within an oval green laurel wreath. This flag, carried during the Peninsular Campaign, became the headquarters flag of the 2d Division, Provisional V Corps, in May 1862 when the brigade was made part of that corps.

Hospitals were distinguished by a yellow flag. As described above, hospital flags were also marked with a Roman letter H in green, and small rectangular guidons of yellow edged with green were used to mark the way from the front line to the field hospitals. Subsistence depots were designated by a green flag.

These flags were attached to a portable staff 14 feet long, in two joints, and were supposed to be habitually displayed in front of the headquarters which they designated. On the march they were to be carried near the unit commander.

These orders were modified by General Orders No. 110, March 26, 1862:

"Third Army Corps: National flag with a small square red and blue (instead of blue and red) flag, vertical, beneath."

"Fourth Army Corps: National flag with a small square red and blue (instead of blue and red) flag, horizontal, beneath."

They were further modified in General Orders No. 119, April 30, 1862, which gave the cavalry reserve headquarters a yellow flag 6 ft. long and 5 ft. wide, with two blue stripes 6 inches in width, crossing diagonally. The reserve's first brigade had a yellow flag the same size, with one blue star in the

A pair of regimental colors in action, June 27, 1862, during the Peninsular Campaign. The national color is topped with an eagle while the regimental color has a spike finial. They are both carried in the front and center of the regimental front.

The regimental color of the 1st Veteran Reserve Corps Regiment conforms in design to those made by Longly & Bros. under Quartermaster Department contract through the Cincinnati Depot. The 18th Veteran Reserve Corps Regiment regimental color, however, was made by Horstmann Bros. for the Philadelphia Depot and differs slightly in design. (West Point Museum Collections)

between brigades quite often, meaning that they had to change flags just as often. Moreover, there was bound to be less loyalty to such an arbitrary and abstract flag than to the elaborate regimental and national colors which were distinguished with the unit's actual designation. Even so, there are a number of surviving examples of regimental designating flags, so many must have seen actual use.

On November 25, 1862, after the V Corps was added to the Army of the Potomac, Brigadier-General Daniel Butterfield of that corps wrote to army headquarters: "In the order designating flags for Army Corps (orders 102 and 110, Headquarters, Army of the Potomac, March 1862) no flag has been designated for the Fifth Corps.

"I would respectfully request that a flag be designated as shown in the following sketch. For the Fifth Army Corps, viz: Red with a Greek Cross in the center, under the national flag as per General Orders No. 102, Army of the Potomac, and that the Quartermaster's Department be directed to furnish the same."

Butterfield's sketch did not in fact show a Greek cross, but a cross *botonée*, which is a form of Greek cross except that each arm ends in a trefoil bud.

On February 7, 1863, according to General Orders No. 10, the corps headquarters flags were

center, while the second brigade had the same flag with two blue stars in the center. The artillery reserve headquarters received a similar sized red flag with a white star in the center, while the brigade of regular infantry received a blue flag of the same size with a white star in the center.

An additional flag was made regulation by General Orders No. 152, August 9, 1862: "The main (ordnance) depot for the army will be designated by a crimson flag, marked 'Ordnance Depot, U.S.A.'"

Although the system was all-inclusive, there is some question as to what degree it was actually practiced. Regiments tended to get transferred

The regimental color bearers for the 111th Pennsylvania Volunteer Infantry Regiment. At the end of the war it was quite popular for units to have their colors photographed so that members could keep the images as mementos of their service. Note the spearpoint finial on the regimental color. (Ronn Palm Collection)

A pre-1863 regimental color for the 5th US Artillery Regiment, with the design smaller in the field than after 1863. (West Point Museum Collections)

changed to blue swallow-tailed guidons 6 ft. on the fly by 2 ft. on the hoist, each with a white cross bearing the corps number in red Roman numerals in the center of the cross. According to the order, the cross was to be a "Maltese cross," but actual examples show it to have been the cross *botonée* that Butterfield, who designed the corps badges, later used in the Army of the Potomac, earlier suggested for the V Corps.

When Major-General Joseph Hooker took over the demoralized Army of the Potomac after the defeat at Fredericksburg and its "mud march," he began to restore the army's morale. In part he did this through a system of badges unique to each division of each corps, worn on the soldier's hat or coat breast. These unique badges were adapted to a revised system of identification flags carried by divisions and brigades which was made official by General Orders No. 53, dated May 12, 1863.

The cavalry corps headquarters was now to carry a flag of the same size and shape as had been used by infantry corps, but all in yellow with white crossed sabers on its center. The artillery reserve headquarters flag was to be the same, but in red with white crossed cannons in its center.

Each division headquarters was to fly a different style flag. Each corps' first division was to have a white rectangular flag with a red corps badge in its center; the second division had a blue flag with a white corps badge; the third, a white flag with a blue corps badge.

The VI Corps' "light division" had a white rectangular flag, with a green Greek cross in its center.

The brigades in each corps' first division had a white triangular flag with a red corps badge in the center. The first brigade simply carried this color; the second brigade had an additional 6-inch-wide blue stripe next to the staff; the third, a 4½-inch blue border all around the flag. According to Billings, "Whenever there was a fourth brigade, it was designated by a triangular block of color in each corner of the flag."

The brigades of each corps' second division had a blue triangular flag with a white corps badge in the center. The individual brigade flags used the same system as in the first division, the stripes and borders being red instead of blue.

The brigades of each corps' third division had a white triangular flag with a blue corps badge in the center. Individual brigade flags used the same system as the first division, the stripe and borders being red.

Although not mentioned in the initial order, soon after it was issued corps artillery headquarters adopted a red brigade flag with the corps badge in white in its center. The corps quartermaster's headquarters had a blue swallow-tailed guidon the same size as the brigade flags with diagonal white stripes parallel with the swallow tails and ending at the top and bottom of the flag at the staff.

This system of flags to designate specific headquarters in the Army of the Potomac continued in use through the army's existence.

Corps Badges of the Army of the Potomac, 1863

Corps	Badge
I	A sphere
II	A trefoil
III	A lozenge
V	A Maltese cross
VI	A (Greek) cross
IX*	A shield with a figure 9 in the center, crossed with a fouled anchor and cannon
X*	A four-bastioned fort
XXI*	A crescent, points up
XII*	A five-pointed star

(*Served with the Army of the Potomac at one time or another but was not always a member of that army.)

The IX Corps adopted a fairly complicated badge which did not lend itself to the simple outline style of badge used by the other corps. It involved a cannon crossing a fouled anchor on a shield. Therefore, when the IX Corps adopted its flags to conform with the Army of the Potomac system on August 1, 1864, it called for flags that were slightly more elaborate than those used by the other corps. The headquarters' blue swallow-tailed guidon had a white shield with a red cannon crossing a blue anchor. The first division's blue shield had a blue cannon crossing a white anchor; the second division's white shield had a red cannon crossing a blue anchor; and the third division's blue shield had a white cannon crossing a red anchor.

Toward the end of the war, casualties forced units to be merged, even at corps level. On November 26, 1864, the merger of troops of the remainder of I Corps into Third Division, V Corps resulted in General Orders No. 10 which read in part, "The Division flag will be the flag now authorized, with a circular belt surrounding the corps, insignia and of the same color."

On March 25, 1864, the First Division, III Corps became the Third Division, II Corps, and the Second Division, III Corps became the Fourth Division, II Corps. However, Major-General A. A. Humphries, last commander of II Corps, later wrote, "No power on earth could consolidate or fuse the Third with the Second, and the authorities were at length compelled to let the Old Third wear their Old Third insignia. The men would not discard the Lozenge or Diamond, and Mott's division headquarters flag, The Old Third, bore a white Trefoil on a blue Diamond or Lozenge on its swallow-tail."

The Army of the James

The Army of the James was created on April 2, 1864, under Major-General Benjamin F. Butler with the purpose of attacking Richmond from the South. It was created with the X and XVIII Corps, which were discontinued on December 3, 1864, when the XXIV and XXV Corps replaced them.

On May 3, 1864, Army headquarters set up a fairly simple system of flag identification through division level. Headquarters used a 6 ft.-square flag divided horizontally red over blue; a large white five-pointed star was placed centrally on the field. The two colors in the field represented the two corps under its command.

According to an order sent to the X Corps commander on May 3, 1864, from the headquarters of the Department of Virginia and North Carolina:

A post-war Quartermaster Department illustration of the regulation artillery regimental color.

The regimental color of the 1st US Artillery Regiment fits the style of colors made in 1863 and afterward. (West Point Museum Collections)

The standard of the 2d US Cavalry Regiment.
(West Point Museum Collections)

"By direction of the commanding general of the department, I have the honor to submit the following explanation of the battle-flags to be used by the troops of this command during the coming campaign: The flag carried by department headquarters will be 6 feet square, two horizontal bars, upper bar red, lower bar blue, with a white star in the center; the flag carried by the headquarters Eighteenth Army Corps will be 6 feet square, blood red, with number '18' in the center; First Division flag, same size, blood red, with a single white star in the center; Second Division flag, same size and color, with two white stars in the center; Third Division flag, same size and color, with three white stars in the center. The flag carried by the Tenth Army Corps will be 6 feet square, dark blue, with the number '10' in the center; First Division flag, same size and color, with a single white star in the center; Second Division flag, same size and color, with two white stars in the center; Third Division, same size and color, with three white stars in the center. Brigade colors will be furnished as soon as practicable."

This system was abandoned when the XXIV and XXV Corps replaced the original corps in the Army. Both of these corps used Army of the Potomac-style headquarters flags: dark blue swallow-tailed guidons, with a white corps badge and the corps number in red Roman numerals. The XXIV Corps badge was a heart, while that of the XXV Corps was a square. Their division flags were the same as in the Army of the Potomac at that time: white for the first and third divisions, and dark blue for the second division. The corps badge was placed on the field of each, red in the first division, white in the second division, and blue in the third division. Flag sizes in the two corps, however, varied. Division flags in the XXIV Corps were 4 ft. 6 ins. on the hoist by 6 ft. In the XXV Corps they were only 2 ft. 7 ins. by 5 ft. 9 ins.

The Department of the Cumberland

On December 19, 1862, General Orders No. 41 was issued by the headquarters XIV Corps and the Department of the Cumberland in Nashville, Tennessee, which divided the forces in the department into "the center" or "wings." Brigades and divisions were assigned into these groups to be numbered from right to left, although referred to by commanders' names in operational reports.

The same order indicated a system of flags to identify the headquarters of these commands:

"III. Flags will be used to indicate the various headquarters, as follows: General headquarters – the National flag, 6 feet by 5, with a golden eagle below the stars, 2 feet from tip to tip. Right wing – a plain light crimson flag. Center – a plain light blue flag. Left wing – a plain pink flag. First Division, right wing – the flag of the wing, with one white star, 18 inches in diameter, the inner point 1 inch from the staff. Second Division, right wing – the flag of the wing, with two white stars, each 18 inches in diameter, the inner points 1 inch from the staff. Third Division, right wing – the flag of the wing, with three white stars, each 18 inches in diameter, set in triangular form, the outside star 1 inch from the outer line of flag. The division flags of the center and left wing will correspond with the above; that is to say, they will be the flags of the center or left wing, as the case may be, and with one, two, or three white stars, each 18 inches in diameter, according as they represent the First, Second, or Third Divisions. The headquarters flags of all brigades will be the flags of their divisions, with the number of the brigade in black, 8 inches long, in the center of each star. That of the brigade of regulars, however, will, instead of the white star and black number, have simply a golden star. The flags of the wings will be 6 feet on staff by 4 feet fly; those of divisions and brigades 5 feet by 3. They will all be of a pattern to be furnished to the quartermaster's department. Artillery reserve – a plain red flag, equilateral in shape, each side being 5 feet. Cavalry reserve – of the same shape as division flags, 3 feet fly by 5 on the staff, but of deep orange color. Divisions and brigades to be designated as in the infantry; that is, the First, Second, and Third Divisions by one, two, and three white stars respectively; the First, Second, and Third Brigades by black figures in each star. Engineer Corps – a white and blue flag, blue uppermost and running horizontally. Flag 5 feet on staff by 3 feet fly. Hospitals and ambulance depots – a light yellow flag, 3 feet square, for the hospitals and for the principal ambulance depot on a field of battle; 2 feet square for the lesser ones. Subsistence depots or store-houses – a plain light green flag, 3 feet square. Quartermaster's depots or store houses – same flag, with the letters QM.D. in white, 1 foot long.

"IV. All of these flags will be attached to a portable staff, 14 feet long, made in two joints, and will be habitually displayed in front of the tent, or from some prominent part of the house or vessel occupied by the officer, whose headquarters they are intended to designate; and on the march will be carried near his person."

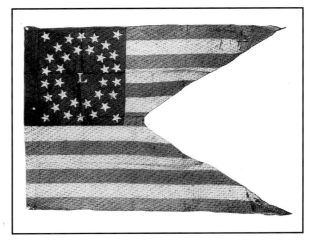

Charging cavalrymen in 1864 carry regulation guidons.

A regulation cavalry guidon carried by an L Troop. (West Point Museum Collections)

This system apparently failed, for General Orders No. 91, issued by the Department of the Cumberland headquarters on April 25, 1863, stated:

"It having been found that the flags prescribed by General Orders, No. 41, from this headquarters, December 19, 1862, to designate the headquarters of the various brigades, divisions, and corps of this army, are not sufficiently marked to be readily distinguished from each other, those herein described will be substituted.

General headquarters The national flag, 6 feet by 5, with a golden eagle below the stars, 2 feet from tip to tip.

Fourteenth Army Corps A bright blue flag, 6 feet by 4, fringed, with black eagle in center, 2 feet from tip to tip, with the number '14' in black on shield, which shall be white.

Twentieth Army Corps A bright red flag, same as that for Fourteenth Army Corps, except the number on the shield, which shall be that of the corps.

Twenty-first Army Corps A bright red, white, and blue flag (horizontal), same as that for Fourteenth Corps, except the number on the shield, which shall be that of the corps.

First Division, Fourteenth Army Corps The flag of the corps, except the eagle and fringe, with one black star, 18 inches in diameter, point 2 inches from staff.

Second Division, Fourteenth Army Corps The flag of the corps, except eagle and fringe, with two black stars, each 18 inches in diameter, inner point 2 inches from staff.

Third Division, Fourteenth Army Corps The flag of the corps, except eagle and fringe, with three black stars, each 18 inches in diameter, set equally along staff, the inner point being 2 inches from staff.

Fourth Division, Fourteenth Army Corps The flag of the corps, except eagle and fringe, with four black stars, each 18 inches in diameter, three of them along staff as before, the other set equally on the flag.

Fifth Division, Fourteenth Army Corps The flag of the corps, except eagle and fringe, with five black stars, each 18 inches in diameter, three of them along the staff, the other two equally distributed on flag.

The division flags of the Twentieth and Twenty-first Army Corps will correspond with the above, that is, the corps flags (without eagle and fringe), with one, two, three, &c., stars, according as they represent the first, second, third, &c., divisions.

The headquarters flags of all brigades will be the flags of their divisions, with the number of the brigade in white, 8 inches long, in center of each star.

The Regular brigade will have the corps and division flag, but the stars shall be golden instead of black.

Artillery reserve Two bright red flags, each 4 feet by 2, one above the other.

Batteries Each battery shall have a small flag, corps

This regulation cavalry guidon was carried by the Cleveland Guards, officially known as L Troop, 1st Rhode Island Cavalry Regiment. (North Carolina Museum of History)

The 1864 headquarters flag of the Department of the Cumberland measures 4 by 4½ ft. The painted eagle is gold, as are the letters "D.C." (West Point Museum Collections)

colors, and arrangement (but 1 foot 6 inches on staff, by 2 feet fly), with the letters and numbers of the battery inscribed thereon in black, 4 inches long, thus, 'B, First Ohio.'

Cavalry headquarters A bright red, white, and blue flag, 6 feet by 4, colors running vertically, red outermost.

First Cavalry Division A bright red, white, and blue flag, 6 feet by 4, like last, with one star, 18 inches in diameter, black, the point 2 inches from staff.

Second Cavalry Division Same as last, except two black stars, each 18 inches in diameter.

"As for infantry, the headquarters flags of brigades will be the flags of divisions, with the number of the brigade in black, 8 inches long.

Engineer Corps A white and blue flag, blue uppermost, and running horizontally, 6 feet by 4.

Hospitals and ambulance depots A light yellow flag, 3 feet by 3, for hospitals and the principal ambulance depot on the field of battle, 2 feet square for the lesser ones.

Subsistence depots and storehouses A plain light green flag, 3 feet square.

Quartermaster's depots or storehouses Same flag, with letters Q.M.D. in white, 1 foot long.

Ordnance department, general headquarters A bright green flag, 3 feet square, with two crossed cannons in white, set diagonally in a square of 3 feet, with a circular ribbon of 6 inches wide and 3 feet greatest diameter (or diameter of inner circle 2 feet), with the letters 'U.S. Ordnance Department,' in black, 4 inches long, on ribbon, and a streamer above flag, 1 foot on staff by 4 feet long, crimson color, with words 'Chief of Ordnance' in black, 6 inches long.

Division ordnance Same flag, with cannon and ribbon, but no streamer."

The XIX Corps

The XIX Corps included all the troops stationed in the Department of the Gulf between January 5, 1863, and March 20, 1865. On February 18, 1863, Department headquarters issued General Orders No. 17 which designated unique flags within the Corps:

"III. The various headquarters of the Department of the Gulf will be designated by small flags or guidons, 4 feet square, attached to a lance 12 feet long, made in two joints, as follows:

"The headquarters of the Nineteenth Army Corps and the Department of the Gulf by a flag, with a white four-pointed star in the center; the figure 19, in red, in the star.

"Division headquarters, red, with a white four-pointed star in the center; the number of the division in black figures in the star.

"Brigade headquarters, blue, white and horizontal stripes of equal width, the number of the brigade in black figures in the white stripes."

General Orders No. 11, dated November 17, 1864, indicated both the corps badge and a unique set of flags for the XIX Corps:

"The flags will be as follows: For the headquarters of the corps, blue swallow-tail, seventy-two inches in length by thirty-nine on staff, with white cross eighteen inches square. For the headquarters of divisions, triangular, sixty-six inches in length by

William McIlvaine, a soldier in the Army of the Potomac, sketched the headquarters of General Andrew Humphreys, 3d Division, V Corps, near Falmouth, Virginia, on March 30 ,1863. The identifying flag made regulation by General McClellan is on the smaller flagpole. It is halved red and blue, the red towards the hoist and the blue towards the fly. (National Archives)

1: National Color, 3d US Inf. Regt.

2: National Color, 1st Bn., 11th US Inf. Regt.
3: Regimental Color, 6th US Inf. Regt.

A

1: Regimental Color, 164th NY Inf. Regt.
2: Standard, 2d US Cav. Regt.
3: Regimental Color, 5th US Arty. Regt.
4: Regimental Color, artillery

1

3

2

4

B

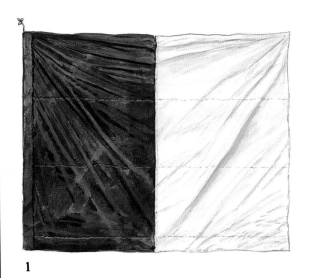

1

3

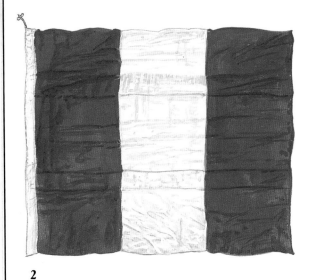

2

4

Designating flags, Army of the Potomac
1: 1st Bde., 2d Div. of a Corps
2: 3d Bde., 1st Div. of a Corps
3: 1st Bde., 4th Div. of a Corps
4: 11th Penn. Volunteer Inf. Regt.

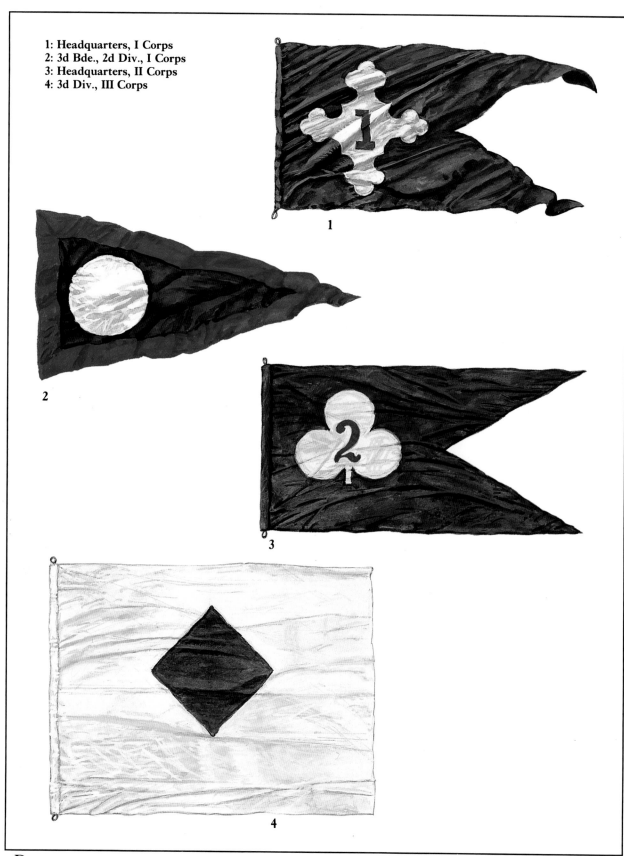

1: Headquarters, I Corps
2: 3d Bde., 2d Div., I Corps
3: Headquarters, II Corps
4: 3d Div., III Corps

D

1: 2d Div., V Corps
2: 1st Div., VI Corps
3: Headquarters, IX Corps
4: Headquarters, X Corps

E

1

1: Headquarters, XXIV Corps
2: Headquarters, XXIII Corps
3: Headquarters, XV Corps
4: 2d Div., XVIII Corps

3

2

4

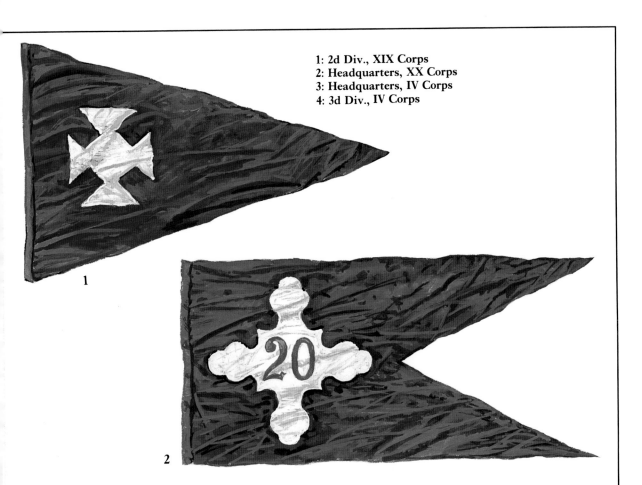

1: 2d Div., XIX Corps
2: Headquarters, XX Corps
3: Headquarters, IV Corps
4: 3d Div., IV Corps

1

2

3

4

1: Co., I, 6th Penn. Cavalry
2: Headquarters, XXI Corps
3: Headquarters, Cavalry Corps, Army of the Potomac

H

This elaborate flag marks the headquarters of the 2d Brigade, 4th Division, IX Corps, and dates from 1864. Its stripes are, from hoist, green, blue, and red, with a red number "2" and a white shield. The anchor is blue and the cannon red. It measures 2½ by 4 ft. (West Point Museum Collections)

forty-four in staff, with cross fifteen inches square. First Division, red, with white cross; Second Division, blue, with white cross; Third Division, white, with blue cross. For the headquarters of brigade, rectangular, thirty-six inches in length by thirty on staff with cross fifteen inches square. First Brigade, First Division, blue and white, horizontal (blue underneath), red cross; Second Brigade, First Division, blue and red, horizontal (blue underneath), with cross; Third Brigade, First Division, red and white, horizontal (red underneath), blue cross; First Brigade, Second Division, blue and white, perpendicular (blue on staff), red cross; Second Brigade, Second Division, blue and red, perpendicular (blue on staff), white cross; Third Brigade, Second Division, red and white, perpendicular (red on staff), blue cross; Fourth Brigade, Second Division, blue and red, perpendicular (red on staff), white cross; First Brigade, Third Division, blue and white, diagonal (blue on staff), red cross; Second Brigade, Third Division, blue and red, diagonal (blue on staff), white cross; Third Brigade, Third Division, red and white, diagonal (red on staff), blue cross."

The XXIII Corps

The XXIII Corps, created April 27, 1863, from troops in Kentucky in the Department of Ohio, also served in the Department of North Carolina until disbanded August 1, 1865. Special Field Orders No.

121, September 25, 1864, stated that:

"The badge of the Twenty-third Corps is an escutcheon in the form of the heraldic shield, all of whose proportions are determined by the width, as follows: The sides of the shield are straight from the top for the distance of one-fourth the width of the shield. Each curved side is struck with the center at the lower point of the straight part of the opposite side and with a radius equal to the width...

"The flags of the corps are as follows: For corps headquarters, a blue flag with a shield in the center of the form prescribed; the body of the shield divided into three panels, one panel at each principal angle of the shield; the upper left-hand panel red, the upper right-hand panel white, the lower panel blue, the whole surrounded by a gold outline one-twelfth as wide as the shield. For headquarters Second Division, the whole of the interior of the shield white, otherwise the same as the corps flag. For headquarters Third Division, the whole of the interior of the shield blue, otherwise the same as the corps flag. For brigade headquarters, a flag similar to the division flag, but with smaller shields along the inner margin corresponding in number to the brigade. The artillery will wear the badge of the division to which the different batteries are respectively attached."

According to one of its members, Major-General Jacob D. Cox, writing in 1887, the system of corps-wide flags lasted throughout the corps' existence.

Although this Army of the Potomac headquarters flag would appear to be that of the 2d Division, I Corps, with a white disc on a blue field, there is no explanation for it being in the headquarters of Brigadier-General Samuel W. Crawford, who commanded the 3d Division, V Corps when this photograph was taken in 1864. The old I Corps merged into the 2d and 4th Divisions, V Corps, in March 1864. (US Army Military History Institute)

"The Corps Headquarters flag was a silk banner of dark Army blue color, with gold fringe, and the corps badge emblazoned in the center. The Division Headquarters flags were, 1st Division, Blue silk banner, yellow worsted fringe, the shield with the same shape as the corps shield in outline & panels, but the panels red in the gold outline. 2d Division, Similar to the last with all the panels white. 3d Division. Similar to last, with all the panels blue. The 3d Div. flag shows only the gold frame of the shield, the panels being of the same blue silk as the flag.

"The Brigade Headquarters flags were of blue bunting without any fringe. They were of the same style of shield as the division flags, but the shield smaller, & instead of being placed in the center of the flag, as many shields used indicated the number of the brigade, and they were placed in the corner of the flag where the Union Jack [sic] is in the National flag:

Shields: 1st Div. Yellow frame, red panels; 2d Div. Yellow frame, white panels; 3d Div. Yellow frame, blue panels. The yellow frame of the shields on the brigade flags was usually made by tenacious yellow paint, the panels being of the red, white, or blue bunting, inserted in the blue flag."

Third Division, Department of West Virginia

According to General Orders No. 7, issued March 23, 1864, by the headquarters, Third Division, Department of West Virginia: "I. Hereafter flags will

The headquarters flags of the II Corps in 1863. (Billings, Hardtack and Coffee)

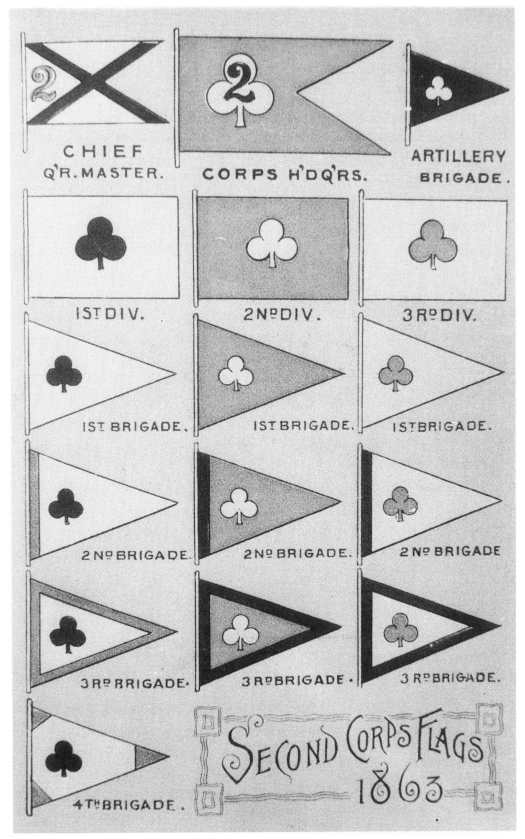

CHIEF Q'R. MASTER.

CORPS H'DQ'RS.

ARTILLERY BRIGADE.

1ST DIV.

2ND DIV.

3RD DIV.

1ST BRIGADE.

1ST BRIGADE.

1ST BRIGADE.

2ND BRIGADE.

2ND BRIGADE.

2ND BRIGADE

3RD BRIGADE.

3RD BRIGADE.

3RD BRIGADE.

4TH BRIGADE.

SECOND CORPS FLAGS 1863

be used to designate the different headquarters of this division, as follows.

"For the division: A three-striped red, white, and blue flag – the stripes to be of width, running diagonally from top to bottom – red at top and white in center, five feet on the staff and six feet fly. The division to be designated by three blue stars thirteen inches long on the white field, the inner corner of which to be five and one-half inches from the staff.

"The brigade flags will be the same as that of the division, with the number of the Brigade in white, six inches long, in the center of each star. These flags to be attached to portable staffs twelve feet long, in two joints, and in the field will be displayed at the quarters of the officers whose headquarters it is intended to designate, and on the march, will be carried near that person."

CAVALRY FLAGS

Originally, Union forces divided cavalry units up among corps, which were largely infantry with artillery support. However, combat soon taught them that cavalry was best used independently; and each army soon adopted cavalry corps, marked by their own flags.

According to General Orders No. 119, April 30, 1862, in the Army of the Potomac, the Cavalry Reserve headquarters was to have a yellow rectangular flag with a blue St. Andrew's cross; the 1st Brigade, a blue star; and the 2d Brigade, two stars. General Orders No. 53, May 12, 1863,

Major-General Winfield Scott Hancock, wearing a hat and with one hand on the tree, stands in front of the headquarters flags of the II Corps, the blue swallow-tail flag and a smaller national color. (US Army Military History Institute)

gave a yellow swallow-tailed guidon with white crossed sabers to the Cavalry Corps headquarters. Its formations used guidons of their own design, although most were made in the regulation horizontally halved form, red over white, with the division number in the opposite color on each bar. Other units divided their guidons into three triangles – white on the hoist, blue on the top, and red on the bottom. A pair of crossed sabers was applied to the white triangle, while gold stars were often painted in the other two.

On August 1, 1864, a full system of Army of the Potomac Cavalry Corps colors was approved. It was very similar to those used by the Army's other corps, with crossed sabers substituted for the corps badges, complete with a dark blue swallow-tailed guidon for the corps headquarters, white and blue rectangular

This 1864 drawing shows two III Corps headquarters flags, that of the corps headquarters and the white flag with either a red lozenge for the 1st Division or a blue lozenge for the 3d Division.

flags for the division headquarters, and pointed guidons for brigades.

On April 26, 1864, General Orders No. 62, Department of the Cumberland, prescribed a system of flags for its cavalry corps. The corps headquarters had a red, white, and blue flag similar to the French tricolor, with a large pair of gold crossed sabers extending over all three bars, and fringed in gold. The first and third divisions had white rectangular flags, the first with red crossed sabers and a blue number 1, the third with blue crossed sabers and a red number 3. The second

37

Battle honors were often placed on headquarters flags as well as unit flags, although this was not strictly according to orders. This photograph of Major-General David B. Birney, who commanded the 1st Division, III Corps (bottom, center, with two medals on his chest), shows both the corps headquarters flag and the division headquarters flag. The latter has battle honors, one for Chancellorsville to the right of the lozenge, painted on it in scrolls. (US Army Military History Institute)

division had a blue flag with white crossed sabers and a red number 2. Brigades received guidons generally following the Army of the Potomac corps flag system.

General Orders No. 3, March 24, 1864, in the Cavalry Corps, Military Division of the Mississippi, produced a different system of flags for that corps' seven divisions. All of its formations had swallow-tail guidons, that for the headquarters being red with yellow crossed sabers, while the divisions had white guidons with dark blue crossed sabers and the division number in red both above and below the sabers.

NAVAL FLAGS

Each commissioned ship of the US Navy and US Marine Revenue Cutter Service flew several flags. A jack, which was simply the dark blue canton with its white stars of the National Flag, was flown at the jack staff of the vessel's bow. A National Flag was flown from different staffs, according to the type of vessel; and a commission pennant identified the ship as a vessel of war. This was a long narrow flag, of blue with a line of white stars at the hoist, and two stripes, red above white.

A contemporary illustration of the V Corps headquarters flag and one of its division headquarters flags. The headquarters flag marked with the backwards "C" is probably intended to have a "6" for the VI Corps.

Captains in command of squadrons, and later admirals, were entitled to fly (or "wear" as it was then termed) a plain blue flag with as many white stars as there were states. In the case of several squadrons merging, the senior officer would use the blue flag while the next in rank had a red flag. If there was a third captain commanding a squadron in the group, he was entitled to fly the same flag in white.

In February 1865 the admiral's flag was changed from square to rectangular.

THE PLATES

A1: National Color, 3d US Infantry Regiment, 1861

The national color carried by the country's oldest continuously serving infantry regiment, the 3d, was made under federal contract through the Philadelphia Depot. It displays one of three known patterns of stars in its canton. The lower star is missing from the lower ring in the 34-star variety,

while the 35-star variety has no central star but has 21 stars in the outer ring.

A2: National Color, 1st Battalion, 11th US Infantry Regiment, 1863

This is a Tiffany & Company, New York, presentation national color with typical script – embroidered unit designation and battle honors. According to tradition, this color was presented on February 22, 1862; the battle honor for Gettysburg (July 1–3, 1863) would indicate that this is incorrect. Apparently the 11th through 19th US Infantry Regiments, which had three battalions, issued regimental colors for their first two battalions, which usually served apart (although probably also to their third battalions, which served as depots if, as few were, they were even organized).

Brigadier-General Charles Griffin (standing with open coat and slouch hat) commanded the I Division, V Corps, in late 1863 when this photograph was taken. The headquarters flag is white with red Maltese cross. (US Army Military History Institute)

A3: Regimental Color, 6th US Infantry Regiment, 1863

The 6th Infantry's regimental color was a Cincinnati Depot federal contract model, believed made by John Shilleto of that city. He received orders for five infantry regimental, two artillery regimental and five national colors on November 3, 1862. Some varieties of these flags have different numbers of stars, yet all have an upper arc that overlaps the end of the motto scroll.

B1: Regimental Color, 164th New York Infantry Regiment, 1864

This flag was supplied under a New York Depot federal contract. Similar colors display 34 stars; these have only 16 stars in the lower arc.

B2: Standard, 2d US Cavalry Regiment, 1861

Cavalry standards were smaller than those carried by foot regiments for two reasons: there was not as much need for unit identification of mounted units on the field as for foot units; and, the larger the flag, the more difficult it was to carry on the march or in action.

B3: Regimental Color, 5th US Artillery Regiment, 1862

Cords and tassels on artillery colors were red and yellow intermixed silk, and crossed cannons replaced the national eagle shown on infantry colors. The colors were also the same size for both infantry and artillery regiments.

B4: Regimental Color, artillery, 1864

In 1863 the design on the artillery regimental color was enlarged to fill more of the field. This particular color was made under a New York Depot federal contract. Often partially decorated scrolls were placed on a color issued to a regiment, which would then be responsible for having the number filled in. This was true of infantry as well as artillery colors.

C1: Designating flag, 1st Brigade, 2d Division of a Corps; Army of the Potomac, 1862

Under the 1862 system of designating flags issued in the Army of the Potomac, each first brigade of a second division, regardless of corps, was to carry this blue and white flag, which measured 5 ft. by 6 ft. This actual flag is in the collection of the US Army Military Academy Museum, West Point, New York. It measures 58 inches at the hoist by 72 inches in the fly.

C2: Designating flag, 3d Brigade, 1st Division of a Corps, Army of the Potomac, 1862

This is another surviving example of an 1862 Army of the Potomac designating flag. This one, which measures 60 inches by 72 inches, is in the New York State Collection.

C3: Designating flag, 1st Brigade, 4th Division of a Corps; Army of the Potomac, 1862

This designating flag, now in the West Point collection, was probably carried in Ord's Division of the Department of the Rappahannock. It measures 54 inches by 70 inches.

C4: Designating flag, 11th Pennsylvania Volunteer Infantry Regiment, 1862

The colors and number on this flag indicate that the unit that carried it was the fourth regiment of the third brigade of the second division, of the III Corps of the Army of the Potomac. In this case, the

This sketch shows the 1st Division, V Corps headquarters flag being carried into battle at Preble's Farm, Virginia, on September 30, 1864

This photograph of X Corps commander Major-General Alfred H. Terry (in the coat with two rows of buttons arranged in threes) shows the standard Army of the Potomac corps headquarters flag being used in that corps instead of the rectangular blue flag bearing a plain number 10 as ordered in the Army of the James. (National Archives)

regiment was the 11th Pennsylvania, which carried this flag in the Second Battle of Manassas.

D1: Headquarters, I Corps, 1863
On February 7, 1863, under General Orders No. 10, all corps headquarters in the Army of the Potomac were to have blue swallow-tailed guidons with a white "Maltese cross" bearing the corps number in red. This odd device, which is not a true Maltese cross by any means, became the standard symbol used. It is actually a cross *botonée*, that is a Greek cross with a trefoil bud at the end of each arm.

D2: 3d Brigade, 2d Division, I Corps, 1863
The Army of the Potomac system of identifying flags adopted on February 7, 1863, gave corps

headquarters a swallow-tailed guidon, with a rectangular flag carried by each division headquarters, and this type of guidon by each brigade headquarters. The white circle is the I Corps badge, which was also worn on soldiers' and officers' headgear and, at times, on the left breast. On August 1, 1864, the corps badge was authorized by General Orders No. 115 to be used on all corps flags.

D3: Headquarters, II Corps, 1864
On August 1, 1864, General Orders No. 115 changed the II Corps headquarters flag by using the assigned Corps badge, a "trefoil," in place of the "Maltese cross." The same device appeared on all this corps' flags, in red for the first division, white for the second division, and blue for the third division. The artillery brigade had a red guidon with a white trefoil, while the corps chief quartermaster had a dark blue swallow-tail guidon with a St. Andrew's cross in white.

D4: 3d Division, III Corps, 1864
Under the system of August 1,1864, all 3d Division,

III Corps flags used a blue corps badge, the lozenge; the 1st and 3d Divisions' headquarters had white flags (with a red lozenge for the 1st Division), while the 2d Division headquarters had a blue flag with a white lozenge. The brigade guidons matched the colors, with the first brigade having plain white, the second having a red stripe at the hoist, the third being bordered in red, and the fourth with red tips. Actually III Corps had been merged into II Corps by the time these flags were ordered, although many did see use until the system was changed by Special Orders No. 320, issued November 24, 1864. The flag of the 3d Division under those orders, now in the New Jersey State Capital, has a white background with a blue trefoil within a red lozenge on the field.

E1: 2d Division, V Corps, 1864

The corps badge of the Army of the Potomac's V Corps was the Maltese cross, which appears in white on its 2d Division's headquarters flag. The V Corps received elements of the old I Corps as the V Corps' 2d and 4th Divisions on March 24, 1864. The old I Corps units were allowed to keep their old corps badges and unit flags; on September 11, 1864, all the I Corps elements were further reduced to the 3d Division, V Corps, complete with their old insignia. On December 20, 1864 a circular ordered all men of the division to wear a "White Maltese Cross" on their hats and all elements of the old I Corps badges were done away with.

E2: 1st Division, VI Corps, 1864

Although originally the Greek cross worn by the VI Corps was ordered to be worn "upright," it appeared as a St. Andrew's cross on a number of headquarters flags carried within the Corps starting in 1864. The Greek cross was carried in the 3d Division; the other divisions used the St. Andrew's cross.

E3: Headquarters, IX Corps, 1864

The IX Corps adopted this unusual corps badge, signifying its service as a landing force along the south-eastern coast, on April 10, 1864. The first Corps headquarters flag used the Army of the Potomac's "Maltese cross" design with a red number 9; it was replaced by a national flag with a corps badge in the canton, surrounded by an oval of stars, in April 1864. This flag was adopted when the Corps was attached to the Army of the Potomac in May

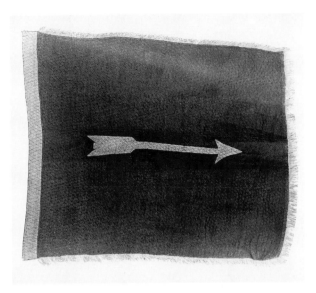

This headquarters flag, in blue with a red arrow and yellow fringe, measures 3½ by 4½ ft., and identified the 1st Division, XVII Corps in 1865. (West Point Museum Collections)

1864, although one source says it was not adopted until August 1, 1864. The divisional flags were red (1st Division), white (2d Division), blue (3d Division), and green (4th Division) with a corps badge of a facing color. Rectangular brigade flags had three vertical stripes with a corps badge and brigade number.

E4: Headquarters, X Corps, 1864

On May 3, 1864, the X Corps adopted square flags for its headquarters and division headquarters. While the number 10 was used on the corps headquarters flags, the divisions had one, two, and three white stars respectively on their blue flags. On May 22, 1864, the Corps' commander wrote: "I have received four flags. I propose to replace the stars on the division flags by the corps badge, which is a square bastioned fort, very like a star in effect, I presume there can be no objection to this." There has been no reply found and, moreover, photographs show the older flag with number 10 in use until the corps' demise in December 1864. Photographs of the recreated corps headquarters, taken after March 1865, show the Army of the Potomac's blue swallowtail guidon with white "Maltese cross" and red number 10 being used.

F1: Headquarters, XXIV Corps, 1865

The corps badge of the XXIV Corps, Department of

Virginia, created from elements of the old X and XVIII Corps, was adopted on March 1, 1865. It consisted of the corps number in red within a white heart. The flag measures 36 inches at the hoist by 72 inches in the fly.

F2: Headquarters, XXIII Corps, 1864

Special Field Orders No. 121, dated September 25, 1864, of the XXIII Corps, Army of the Ohio, read: "The flags of this corps are as follows: For corps headquarters, a blue flag with a shield in the corner

(Left) The flag carried by the Chief Quartermaster, XIX Corps, in 1864-65 featured a red cross on a white disc on a blue field. It measures 2½ ft by 3½ ft. (West Point Museum Collections)

(Right) The headquarters flag of Brigadier-General Hugh Judson Kilpatrick (standing behind seated lady), who commanded cavalry in the Army of the Cumberland, had red and white stripes, with a white disc in the center around an eagle mounted on a national color in natural colors. The word "TUEBOR" was painted in black. The photograph was taken in Stevensburg, Virginia, in March 1864. (US Army Military History Institute)

There are some flags which were clearly made for unit identification but whose purpose is unknown today. This flag, for example, was found among the effects of Thomas Low of Tennessee, who served in the 2d US Tennessee Infantry, which was in the 7th Division in Alabama at one point. It appears to be some sort of identification flag for that unit, but no orders establishing its design have been found. It has a white field, with red stripes along the fly, and blue four-pointed stars, a blue eagle, and blue number 7. (Mike Miner Collection)

of the form prescribed; the body of the shield divided into three panels, one panel at each principal angle of the shield; the upper left-hand panel red, the upper right-hand panel white, the lower panel blue, the whole surrounded by a golden outline one-twelfth as wide as the shield. For headquarters Second Division, the whole of the interior of the shield white, otherwise the same as the corps flag. For headquarters Third Division, the whole of the interior blue, otherwise the same as the corps flag. For brigade headquarters, a flag similar to the division flag, but with smaller shield along the inner margin corresponding in number to the brigade. The artillery will wear the badge of the division to which the different batteries are respectively attached." The 1st Division presumably received the same flag with a red shield on joining the corps in the spring of 1865.

F3: Headquarters, XV Corps, 1865

By General Orders No. 21, dated April 9, 1865, the XV Corps adopted its corps badge of a cartridge box under the motto "FORTY ROUNDS" as the center-piece of its flags. The rectangular flags carried by headquarters and division headquarters were 5 ft. by 5 ft. 6 ins. The division flags were all red for the 1st Division, white for the 2d, blue for the 3d, and yellow for the 4th; the corps headquarters flag was quartered in the three first division colors. Swallow-tailed guidons were carried by brigade headquarters. These measured 4ft. by 5 ft. 6 ins., and came in appropriate division colors with different borders to designate the different brigades. The corps badges on surviving examples have been painted on the fields.

F4: 2d Division, XVIII Corps, 1864

The XVIII Corps, of the Army of the James, first adopted the same type of flags as used in the X Corps, with the corps number in white on the headquarters flag, and one, two, or three stars, according to the division, on each division headquarters flag. Instead of the blue fields of the X Corps, the XVIII Corps used red. However, on June

Major-General David M. Gregg (seated, wearing a slouch hat) commanded the 2d Division, Cavalry Corps, Army of the Potomac. The red and white division headquarters flag is tied to his tent pole. (US Army Military History Institute)

7, 1864, a "cross with foliate sides," similar to the "Maltese cross" used on Army of the Potomac corps headquarters flags, was adopted as the corps badge. A new corps headquarters flag using this device appears to have been taken into use around July 1864.

G1: 2d Division, XIX Corps, 1864

On February 28, 1863, XIX Corps, of the Department of the Gulf, issued its General Orders No. 17 which called for a headquarters flag: "A blue flag with a white four-pointed star, in the center; the number 19, in red, on the star." Each division flag

was "red, with a white four-pointed star, in the center, the number of the division in black figures on the star." General Orders No. 11, November 17, 1864, revised the system to use the corps' newly adopted badge, "a fan-leaved cross with octagonal center." Headquarters used a blue swallow-tailed guidon with a white corps badge, while the guidon used by the 2d Division reversed the colors.

G2: Headquarters, XX Corps, 1864

The XX Corps of the Army of the Cumberland was formed on April 4, 1864, from units of the XXII Corps and the XXI Corps. On April 26 Department of the Cumberland General Orders No. 62 awarded its headquarters a blue swallow-tailed guidon with a white "Tunic cross" and the red number 20. Old XXII Corps flags were used by the division headquarters, with a 6 ft.-square white flag with a blue star in the 3d Division, and a red field with a green star in the 4th Division. Triangular flags, each side being 6 ft. long, were used by brigade headquarters; these followed the Army of the Potomac system for differentiating brigades.

G3: Headquarters, IV Corps, Army of the Cumberland, 1864

The IV Corps of the Army of the Cumberland was different from most corps in that its badge, an equilateral triangle, was not used in any form on the corps flags. Instead, corps and division headquarters used red flags with a blue canton. Headquarters used a golden eagle in its canton.

G4: 3d Division, IV Corps, 1864

Each division of the IV Corps used white stripes to make a design in the blue cantons of their otherwise red flags. The 1st Division had one stripe running diagonally from bottom left to top right; the 2d had a white St. Andrew's cross; and the 3d, a white St. Andrew's cross with a vertical stripe through the middle. Brigades had swallow-tailed guidons with the same canton as their division, but with one, two, or three white stars under the canton according to the brigade number.

H1: Co. I, 6th Pennsylvania Cavalry (Rush's Lancers), 1863

This regulation cavalry guidon was carried by the cavalry company that accompanied the headquarters of the Army of the Potomac during the Battle of Gettysburg. The battle honor for that engagement would therefore suggest that it was carried for some time at least after July 1863. The cavalryman holding the guidon wears the dress jacket worn by mounted troops, trimmed in yellow for cavalry.

H2: Headquarters, XXI Corps, 1863

The oddly shaped XXI Corps flags were prescribed in the Department of the Cumberland's General Orders No. 91, April 25, 1863. The corps headquarters flag, which was 6 ft. in hoist by 4 ft. in the fly, used an eagle with the number 21, while divisions had from one to three stars on the white stripe. Brigades used the division flags, but with the white number of the brigade replacing the star.

H3: Headquarters, Cavalry Corps, Army of the Potomac, 1864

Cavalry in the Army of the Potomac used a variety of systems of flag identification, starting from 1862 when a blue St. Andrew's cross on a yellow field was authorized for the cavalry reserve headquarters. On May 12, 1863, it was authorized a yellow swallow-tailed flag with white crossed sabers in the center. Thereafter most cavalry commands used crossed sabers, the traditional Cavalry Corps badge, on their flags. This headquarters flag was adopted in 1864 and apparently used until the end of the war.

SELECT BIBLIOGRAPHY

Beale, James, *The Battle Flags of the Army of the Potomac at Gettysburg, Penna, July 1st, 2d & 3d, 1863*, Philadelphia, 1885.

Billings, John D., *Hardtack and Coffee*, Glendale, New York, 1970.

Madaus, H. Michael, "McClellan's System of Designating Flags, Spring–Fall, 1862", *Military Collector & Historian*, Washington, DC, Spring 1965, pp1–13.

Madaus, Howard M., "The Conservation of Civil War Flags: The Military Historian's Perspective", *Papers presented at the Pennsylvania Capitol; Preservation Committee Flag Symposium, 1987*, Harrisburg, 1987.

Official, *Atlas to accompany the Official Records ...*, Washington, DC, 1891–1895.

Phillips, Stanley S., *Civil War Corps Badges and Other Related Awards, Badges, Medals of the Period*, Lanham, Maryland, 1982.

Sauers, Richard A., *Advance the Colors!*, Harrisburg, 1987.

Todd, Frederick P., *American Military Equippage*, Vol II, Providence, Rhode Island, 1977.

INDEX

Date Due

MAY 16 '06			
MAR 16 '07			
SEP 24 2008			

BRODART   Cat. No. 23 233   Printed in U.S.A

LIBRARY OF THE
SCHOOL OF THE INCARNATION
2601 SYMPHONY LANE
GAMBRILLS, MD 21054